LIGHTNING BOLT BOOKS™

Let's Visit the Ocean

Jennifer Boothroyd

Lerner Publications • Minneapolis

For the
Bushard family

Lerner Publications Company
A division of Lerner Publishing Group, Inc.
241 First Avenue North
Minneapolis, MN 55401 USA

For reading levels and more information, look up this title at www.lernerbooks.com.

Library of Congress Cataloging-in-Publication Data

Names: Boothroyd, Jennifer, 1972– author.
Title: Let's visit the ocean / Jennifer Boothroyd.
Description: Minneapolis : Lerner Publications, [2017] | Series: Lightning bolts books. Biome explorers | Includes index.
Identifiers: LCCN 2015044359 (print) | LCCN 2016009779 (ebook) | ISBN 9781512411942 (lb : alk. paper) | ISBN 9781512412321 (pb : alk. paper) | ISBN 9781512412024 (EB pdf)
Subjects: LCSH: Ocean—Juvenile literature. | Marine ecology—Juvenile literature.
Classification: LCC GC21.5 .B67 2017 (print) | LCC GC21.5 (ebook) | DDC 577.7—dc23

LC record available at http://lccn.loc.gov/2015044359
Manufactured in the United States of America
1 – BP – 7/15/16

Table of Contents

A Journey to the Ocean

Back and forth, back and forth. Water washes up on a sandy beach. Then it flows back into the ocean.

An ocean is a large body of salt water. The ocean covers most of Earth's surface.

The ocean biome is divided into the Pacific, Atlantic, Indian, Arctic, and Southern Oceans.

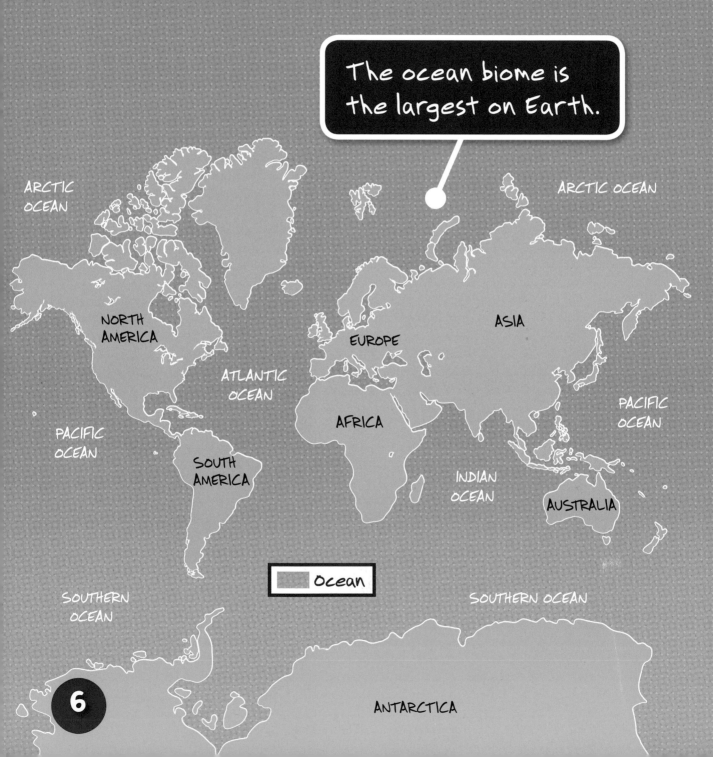

The ocean biome is the largest on Earth.

ARCTIC OCEAN

ARCTIC OCEAN

NORTH AMERICA

EUROPE

ASIA

ATLANTIC OCEAN

PACIFIC OCEAN

AFRICA

PACIFIC OCEAN

SOUTH AMERICA

INDIAN OCEAN

AUSTRALIA

Ocean

SOUTHERN OCEAN

SOUTHERN OCEAN

ANTARCTICA

Parts of the ocean are very deep. Sunlight can't reach the bottom in many areas.

Much of the ocean hasn't been explored. People need special equipment to explore deep underwater.

Animals of the Ocean

The ocean is a habitat for many animals. There are animals all over the ocean, from the surface way down to the deepest bottoms.

There are thousands of different fish in the ocean. They come in many different shapes, colors, and sizes.

Many fish, animals, and plants live around coral reefs.

Coral reefs are made from tiny animals. These animals grow hard skeletons outside their bodies that stick together. The skeletons remain even after the animals have died.

An albatross is a bird that lives on the ocean. It eats fish and drinks salt water from the ocean. Albatrosses glide on strong gusts of wind and float on the water when they need to rest.

The albatross can glide in the air for many hours.

Krill are about 2.5 inches (6 centimeters) long. Krill gather plants to eat with their front legs. Their back legs move them through the water.

Blue whales are found in every ocean on Earth. They come to the surface to breathe air. An adult blue whale can eat up to 4 tons (3.6 metric tons) of krill every day.

Newborn blue whales weigh more than most cars.

Jellyfish float through the water. Jellyfish have tentacles that hang from their bodies. They can sting other animals that become their prey.

Sea turtles live most of their lives in the ocean. Their large flippers help them swim. They come to the surface to breathe air.

Female turtles return to land to lay their eggs.

Plants in the Ocean

Ocean plants are similar to plants on land. They need sunlight to survive. They release oxygen. They provide food and shelter for ocean animals.

Phytoplankton float in the upper layer of the ocean to collect sunlight.

Phytoplankton are tiny ocean plants. These plants are food for many ocean animals.

Many animals use sea grass as food or habitat. Sea grass grows its roots in the ocean floor.

Sea grass is different from seaweed. The two plants grow and get nutrients in different ways.

Kelp forests grow in cold ocean waters. Kelp can grow very tall.

Many animals depend on Kelp for shelter and food.

Kelp is actually a type of algae, not a plant.

Kelp gets nutrients from its leaves instead of roots, like plants usually do. Rootlike objects called holdfasts keep kelp on the ocean floor. Gas pockets help it float toward the light.

Working Together

The ocean is a giant ecosystem. All the living and nonliving parts work together. The ocean also has many smaller ecosystems. One important ecosystem is the rocky shore.

Kelp and phytoplankton grow on the rocks. They are food to many animals.

Sea urchins live in the rocks.
They eat the kelp.

Sea stars used to be called starfish, but they are not fish. They are echinoderms.

Sea stars also live among the rocks. They eat the urchins.

The sea stars help the ecosystem. If there were too many urchins, they would eat all the kelp. Other animals wouldn't have enough food.

The ocean is an amazing biome.
There is so much to explore!

People and the Ocean

People use the ocean in a variety of ways. People visit the ocean to swim or surf the waves. They travel across the ocean in large boats. Many people catch fish or other ocean animals. People need to use the ocean responsibly. People should keep trash and chemicals out of the ocean. Water pollution hurts the plants and animals. People also shouldn't catch too many of the same kinds of fish. This might cause an animal to become extinct.

Biome
Extremes

- Longest wingspan: albatross, 11 feet (3.4 meters)

- Largest animal on Earth: blue whale, 100 feet (30 m) long and 200 tons (181 metric tons)

- Largest fish: whale shark, 39 feet (12 m) and 40 tons (36 metric tons)

- Largest ocean area: Pacific Ocean, more than 60 million square miles (155 million square kilometers)

- Deepest part of the ocean: the Challenger Deep, beneath the western Pacific Ocean, 36,200 feet (11,034 m)

Glossary

biome: plants and animals in a large area, such as a desert or forest

ecosystem: an area of connected living and nonliving things

habitat: the natural home of a plant or animal

holdfast: a rootlike object that holds a single kelp to the ocean floor

nutrient: a substance that is needed by people, animals, and plants to stay healthy and strong

ocean: a large body of salt water covering Earth's surface

oxygen: a gas people and animals need to breathe

phytoplankton: a tiny ocean plant that is too small to see with the naked eye

prey: an animal that is hunted by another animal for food

Further Reading

Duke, Shirley. *Seasons of the Ocean Biome*. Vero Beach, FL: Rourke, 2013.

Fleisher, Paul. *Ocean Food Webs in Action*. Minneapolis: Lerner Publications, 2014.

Hirsch, Rebecca E. *Humpback Whales: Musical Migrating Mammals*. Minneapolis: Lerner Publications, 2015.

Ocean Portal: Smithsonian National Museum of Natural History
http://ocean.si.edu/ocean-photos/what-largest-whale-cetacea-size-comparison-chart

Underwater Forests: Ocean Today
http://oceantoday.noaa.gov/underwaterforests

World Biomes: Kids Do Ecology
http://kids.nceas.ucsb.edu/biomes/marine.html

Index

Photo Acknowledgments

The images in this book are used with the permission of: © Danita Delimont/Alamy, pp. 2, 8; © Pawel Kazmierczak/Shutterstock.com, p. 4; NASA/NOAA/GOES Project, p. 5; © Laura Westlund/Independent Picture Service, p. 6; © Rich Carey/Shutterstock.com, p. 7; © iStockphoto.com/ifish, pp. 9, 10; © Jag_cz/Shutterstock.com, p. 11; © iStockphoto.com/Damerau, p. 12; © Artur Golbert/Alamy, p. 13; © Mark Carwardine/Getty Images, p. 14; © iStockphoto.com/vilainecrevette, p. 15; © Ellen Atkin/Destinations/Design Pics Inc/Alamy, p. 16; © Emmanuel LATTES/Alamy, p. 17; © Scenics & Science/Alamy, p. 18; © WaterFrame/Alamy, p. 19; © NatalieJean/Shutterstock.com, p. 20; © Daniel Poloha/Shutterstock.com, p. 21; © ekipaj/Shutterstock.com, p. 22; © Robert Potsma/Getty Images, p. 23; © Glenn Bartley/All Canada Photos/Alamy, pp. 24, 25, 26; © iStockphoto.com/Predrag Vuckovic, pp. 27, 31.

Front cover: © iStockphoto.com/cdascher.

Main body text set in Johann Light 30/36.